The UNBOUNDED Heart of Grief Relief JOURNAL

RICHARD BALLO

Author of *The Heart of Grief Relief Journal* and *Life without Lisa*

The Unbounded Heart of Grief Relief Journal

Published and Distributed by
Tolman Main Press
5430 Jaeger Road, Suite #201, Naples, FL 34109

The Unbounded Heart of Grief Relief Journal, The Heart of Grief Relief Journal, Life without Lisa, and *The Heart of Grief Relief Kit* are available at special quantity discounts for bulk purchase for sales promotions, premiums, fund-raising and educational needs. Special books or book excerpts also can be created to fit specific needs.

For details, write Tolman Main Press
5430 Jaeger Road, Suite #201, Naples, FL 34109
www.tolmanmainpress.com

ISBN 978-0-9885469-4-3

Editorial services: Jill H. Lawrence, Ruby Slippers, Inc., www.RubySlippersInc.com
Book interior and cover: Dave Aldrich, www.AldrichDesign.com

Neither the publisher nor the author are engaged in rendering professional advice or services to the individual reader. The ideas, procedures and suggestions contained in the book are not intended as a substitute for consulting with your physician or therapist. All matters regarding your physical and mental health require professional and medical supervision. Neither the author nor the publisher shall be liable or responsible for any loss or danger allegedly arising from any information or suggestion in this book.

While the author has made every effort to provide accurate telephone numbers and Internet addresses at the time of publication, neither the publisher nor the author assume any responsibility for errors.

Printed in the U.S.A.

Visit us at www.TolmanMainPress.com, www.RichardBallo.com

DEDICATION

The Unbounded Heart of Grief Relief Journal
is dedicated to art therapists.

Each of us has an artist within us yearning to scream, cry, create, and express our emotions in a visual format that tells the world how we are feeling. Yet, many times we don't want the world to see our creations. Mostly we create for our own emotional, spiritual, and physical healing. We create to represent what we feel when words can no longer tell our story.

Art therapists guide us toward expressions that lead to a new tomorrow and a slate clean of past pains.

Also by Richard Ballo:

Life without Lisa
The Heart of Grief Relief Journal
The Heart of Grief Relief Kit

ACKNOWLEDGEMENTS

THERE ARE MANY PEOPLE TO THANK for their help bringing this journal to life in order to help those dealing with grief.

I would like to thank Jill Lawrence of Ruby Slippers, Inc. for her creativity, ingenuity and tireless work behind the scenes to bring this project to life. Thanks to Debbie Darling for proofreading, and Dave Aldrich of Aldrich Design for his great cover design and interior layout.

The authors and thinkers whose quotes spoke to the heart of grief that I used on the pages of this journal also deserve acknowledgement. Often such words of wisdom and inspiration help take us through the darkest of times. I am grateful to be able to provide a platform to share their words with many who may be bolstered by them.

I would like to thank Avow for their outstanding community service as well as for giving me the opportunity as a volunteer to assist in spreading the word of the hospice mission and, as a result, meeting so many great people. I would also like to thank the doctors, social workers, and authors who believed in this project and gave me support and encouragement.

To my sons Victor and Nick, and my grandchildren, who bring joy to my life and help me, keep life in perspective.

To my wife Terri for her life, love, and laughter.

My heartfelt gratitude goes to all.

Rich Ballo

Rich Ballo

CONTENTS

Use these pages to achieve greater grief relief – Express your grief to feel relief

Let your imagination, mood, and needs of the moment determine how you fill these journal pages. Express your grief your way – be it in words, pictures, drawings, or photos. Each journal page is free of lines and constraints. Your options are unbounded.

The Unbounded Heart of Grief Relief Journal is both a sequel to The Heart of Grief Relief Journal and a stand-alone journal as well. You can begin with this journal or the other. The order is not important, although there are a few differences between the two books. Both journals contain quotes on each journal page to inspire, encourage, support and stir the unbounded expression of your deepest thoughts and feelings during the grieving process.

The Heart of Grief Relief journal contains pages that are lined, but the Unbounded Grief Relief journal's pages are blank except for the quotes. This is intentional because pictures and drawings can also express emotions if you are more inclined to think and express yourself outside the lines.

These unbounded, unstructured pages invite a variety of journal entries that may take different form. Naturally, you will still express your thoughts and feelings, hopes and fears. But now you can also express your feelings by creating montages of drawings, or images you've clipped from magazines. These unlined pages also give you a place to use a technique called "clustering," "mind mapping or naming and framing." (Please see more information regarding these techniques on page XX in the article entitled: Facilitate healing your broken heart by using word association methods like clustering or mind-mapping.)

There are countless benefits that accrue to those who journal on a regular basis. Research has shown that writing words about your process reduces stress, promotes greater self-knowledge and even sparks creativity. If you incorporate gratitude into your journal entries, more research suggests you will end up feeling happy! Yes, happy! AND empowered. So allow yourself to sneak a peek at positive things in your life and quickly write them down before they disappear like snow in the spring. That simple act repeated on a daily basis can be positively life changing in and of itself.

Two dozen research studies show that by expressing one's deepest thoughts and feelings about experiences that are emotionally upsetting, on paper then better mental and physical health result.

We encourage you to use these pages for the highest purpose: helping yourself to recover from your loss and to forge a new, albeit different, life. You can get to unbounded grief relief...these pages will help take you there.

A word from the author, Richard Ballo

Your grief can be softened and shortened if you give full expression to your thoughts, feelings, fears, hopes and dreams

To find peace, contentment and even happiness after suffering the loss of your loved one, just look to your hands. Your hands can play a key role in your recovery; your hands can help you chart a new life and even smile again.

Smile again? Is that even remotely possible, you may be sighing to yourself. I call tell you from firsthand experience, you can and will smile again even if you have suffered the most grievous loss, the deepest despair and desolation. The way back to living, and yes, smiling again, lies in your own hands, both literally and figuratively.

Think about it for a minute. If you put your hands to work using this journal, your hands can create many things, including handwritten words, but also collages of meaningful photos, pictures and even memorabilia like a paper napkin, a piece of fabric, a leaf. These unbounded pages also invite you to draw what you're feeling and wanting to express. The options are endless – unbounded in fact.

Using your hands in these ways can bring you relief and healing despite the intense grief you have been experiencing. You don't have to be an artist either. I am not an artist but I drew images that represented how I felt inside. They were images that I understood and that is the reason to draw: to help yourself.

Express your feelings in words and pictures

Toward that end, I invite and encourage you to pick up a pen or pencil, assemble images, or create them yourself. Express what you're feeling, what you fear, who you are mourning, your loss, and devastation. Express it all in both words and pictures.

This journal offers you the benefit of letting off steam and releasing emotional pressure in a fully safe and therapeutic way. The benefit of that alone cannot be overstated. Journaling provides a personal, private outlet for expressing your most heartfelt concerns and ruminations which in the end, may well transport you to a far better emotional state.

These The Unbounded Heart of Grief Relief Journal pages are here to hold your handwritten words and meaningful images. Not keyboard written words, handwritten. Research now shows that there's some level of disconnecting from emotions when you write using a keyboard vs. handwriting with pen to paper. Handwriting your thoughts and feelings, called expressive journaling, is extremely therapeutic on so many levels. Recently it has been proven that handwriting automatically gives you a laser-like focus and engages various parts of your brain including massive regions involving thinking, language and memory. In fact, The Wall Street Journal reported that writing longhand helps keep minds sharp as they age.

Your journal is your safe haven

But as compelling as these benefits are, the top priority of this journal is to give you a safe place to let it all out, to tell it like it is deep inside you, to give voice and expression to the darkness, the anguish, the feelings of fear that generate hopelessness and helplessness – the two most dangerous and debilitating of all emotional states.

You've come a long way after having filled the pages of the Heart of Grief Relief Journal. Now you can go even further with this one and as many more of these you need.

The famed philosopher William James said, "If you can change your mind, you can change your life." Journaling can help you do just that.

My wife died at 38

My wife and I were in our late thirties when she lost her battle with cancer. I knew I was young enough to live and love again, but knowing that intellectually and feeling that as a real possibility are two different things.

Journaling helped me in the darkest days of my grief. Slowly, piece by piece, my shattered heart came back together again. After a while, I made the conscious decision to live life to the fullest because I am sure Lisa would have wanted me to and as long as I was alive myself, I wanted to enjoy living again. Years later, after I had expressed my thoughts and feelings and received meaningful counseling from Hospice groups and therapists, I was ready to see the possibilities, and ready to accept and give love. One day this amazing woman walked into my life. Because I had tended to my own recovery, I was ready to embrace her and love once again. My healing brought wisdom and experience with it, and as a result, I was able to recognize that she was different. She was the one I had been waiting for and working towards.

Perhaps one of the most famous journalers of all time was 13-year-old Anne Frank. She wrote that she wanted to bring out all kinds of things that lay buried deep in her heart by writing on a regular basis. I wish that for you as well since that kind of delving deep into feelings and thoughts will yield the most impressive, therapeutic results.

Express your thoughts and feelings and then express some more. Day in, day out. And as you do so, your wounds will heal and your life will take on a new, positive dimension as the searing pain of loss is soothed. You will once again invite laugher into your life. And, one day you may notice feeling happy, joyful and fulfilled.

You don't have to believe me. This is not a matter of blind faith. Express fully and completely on these pages in whatever form feels best each day and then notice how the process makes you feel. I had no idea such healing was possible and yet I came from the blackest abyss to create a new life that is a genuine pleasure to live.

Take pen or pencil, photos, drawings and memorabilia in those hands of yours to express it all today, tomorrow and the next day. Write until you've truly expressed it all and said it all. Place images on this journal's pages that evoke feelings and trigger awareness. In these pages, you can also place images of the new life you want to create, too. Knowing what you want is as important as knowing where you are.

Life will be beautiful again. Life will be fulfilling and exciting. Life is waiting for you to embrace it, live it and get on with it. You know your loved one would want it no other way for you.

No one can nor will replace your loved one. That person was unique, special and beloved. But one day someone looking for the same thing in life as you are will walk into your life and take your hand – whether that be a new love, a child that will flourish from your love, a best friend, or a person with strong maternal or paternal instincts. Whatever your life calls out for will be added. Be ready for that person. Do your part by filling up the pages in this journal, and additional journals if need be, and creating your new life. And then expect life to be beautiful again.

I wish you healing, peace and happiness once again. I am living proof that is possible, so take heart. Live each day as best you can, fill these pages and expect happiness to bloom in your life.

Rich Ballo

Richard H. Ballo

Facilitate healing your broken heart by using word association methods like clustering or mind-mapping

THERE ARE NO RULES FOR USING THIS JOURNAL and, in fact, there aren't even any lines to stay within. This journal is called unbounded for a reason – you can express your emotions and feelings in any way your heart desires.

With that said, there are some techniques you might be interested in incorporating during your journey using this journal. That process is called by a number of names including mind mapping, clustering and naming and framing. Whatever you call it, it is basically free-flowing word association without rules, dictates or confines.

Easily get to the heart of the matter and heal your grieving heart

We invite you to consider using such an approach since it will often enable you to truly get to the very heart of the matter easily and effortlessly. Your grief recovery and healing is slowed considerably until you allow yourself to reveal your deepest feelings, fears and concerns. Without doing so, you are merely treading water, making minimal progress if any.

Your left-brain, conscious mind is a wonderful ally. It's the champion "take action, think logically, do it now" linear guidance system. But one of the many things it does so well that probably is not beneficial to you, is to encourage you to look away from painful feelings and memories in order to minimize hurt - an approach that is not very helpful in this case. Your pain and suffering are merely prolonged and more acutely felt using the "if I don't look at that or feel that, I will avoid a lot of pain" approach. The truth is, genuine healing is much more likely to happen when you allow your creative right brain to take over. Word association is right brain driven and can help you get through it all and heal.

Dr. Rico advised the use of clustering to get through your pain

According to Dr. Gabriele Rico, you can use clustering to make your way through pain and crisis. Dr. Rico advises that you begin by drawing a circle on the top third of a journal page. In the middle of this circle, write a word, phrase, issue, problem, or question that happens to pop into your mind. "Pull a word out of thin air if you want to experiment with this technique," she advised prior to her death in 2013.

Once you have put a word or two inside that top circle, let your unbounded thoughts flow. Dr. Rico recommended that as other words and phrases come to mind, write each of them down in its own circle and use arrows to lead from one circle to whatever next one springs to mind.

Don't be surprised when your logical, linear, left-brain mind balks at this process. In fact, it may even "refuse to participate" like a recalcitrant child. But you may be pleasantly surprised to discover that you end up expressing things that your left-brain mind would normally censor in a misguided attempt to protect you. But letting go and allowing the words to find life on paper could prove highly illuminating and healing.

Cluster words, circles and arrows to aid your healing process

For example, you may find the page filled with circles with arrows drawn from circle to circle that reveal your deepest feelings. The top encircled word could be death which leads to heartbreak and onto devastation, to hopelessness, anguish, fear, terror, being abandoned and alone. Dr. Rico advised that "your words will not appear revealing in themselves, but they are the mind's shorthand. They make you aware of a tentative pattern of feeling. Simply begin, on the bottom half of the page, to write what emerges. You will discover feelings that have been brought to the surface by the clustering process."

This type of approach differs from standard journal writing since there is no narrative or loose story line. It's more compressed, much more spontaneous and often feels effortless and flows of its own accord. Insights often follow.

You may wish to do a little researching on clustering, mind mapping or naming and framing. Or just jump right in and give it a try. Whatever you call it, it could be the lynchpin for inner discoveries that will take you more firmly in the direction of unbounded grief relief.

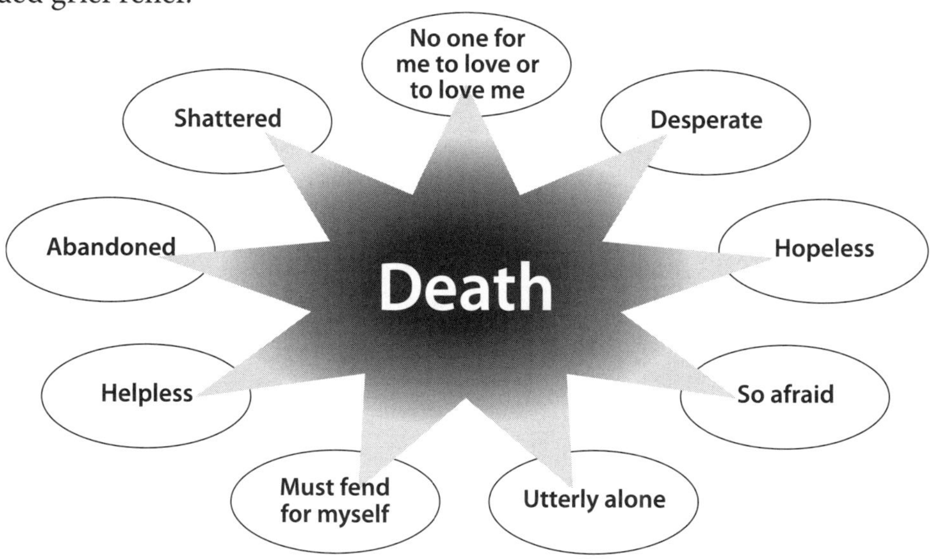

Dr. Gabriele L. Rico authored several books on journaling including *Writing the Natural Way*. Dr. Rico died in 2013, but her website www.gabrielerico.com showcases all her books, and gives examples of the clustering technique.

Proof that journaling can make a profound difference in your life

Countless benefits accrue to those who journal on a regular basis. Research has shown that writing words about your process reduces stress, promotes greater self-knowledge and even sparks creativity. If you incorporate gratitude into your journal entries, more research suggests you will end up feeling happy! Yes, happy! AND empowered. So allow yourself to sneak a peek at positive things in your life and quickly write them down before they disappear like snow in the spring. That simple act repeated on a daily basis can be positively life changing in and of itself. And even in grief we have sightings of happiness.

Two dozen research studies show that by expressing one's deepest thoughts and feelings on paper about experiences that are emotionally upsetting, better mental and physical health result.

Use these journal pages to gain the benefits research proves exist

We encourage you to use these pages for the highest purpose: helping yourself to recover from your loss and to forge a new, albeit different, life. You can get to unbounded grief relief...these pages will help take you there.

The psychologist Ira Progoff discovered in the mid-1960s that an "intensive journal process" could "Draw each person's life toward wholeness at its own tempo..."

Evidence has emerged over the years that proves that people who create thoughtful and emotional journal entries about traumatic experiences improve their physical and psychological health. Perhaps in the aftermath of grief, after the loss of a loved one, such results are especially welcomed.

Boost your immune system by writing and expressing in this journal about the loss of your loved one

Probably the reigning authority on journaling today is James Pennebaker, PhD, who is a psychologist, researcher and professor at the University of Texas at Austin and author of the seminal, Writing to Heal: A Guided Journal for Recovering from Trauma & Emotional Upheaval. Pennebaker reports that regular journaling strengthens immune cells called T-lymphocytes. In addition, research shows that journaling decreases the symptoms of asthma as well as rheumatoid arthritis. Why? Pennebaker's theory is that the act of writing about stressful events such as the loss of a loved one, helps the person who is expressing their feelings and thoughts on paper come to terms with the loss and reduces the negative impact of stress.

Kathleen Adams, founder of The Center for Journal Therapy and author of Journal to the Self, suggests various approaches to help delve deep when journaling. You may want to try a few of her ideas out. She suggests using key phrases that may springboard you into deeper reflection, exploration and expressive writing. Here are some springboards she suggests using: "I am excited about...." "How am I feeling right now?" "I'm happiest when...." "I'm proud of myself for...." "What do I really want?" "My biggest fear is...."

Include your deepest feelings and gain maximum benefit from journaling

Adams also recommends writing about a captured moment in time. For example, write about the day your loved one died, the moment of death or the moment you learned of their death. She says to include all the sensory details surrounding the moment. Write about your feelings that are evoked by this memory. Challenging without question, but highly beneficial in the long run.

Other journal entries Adams says to consider might include a list of twenty-five to fifty things in each of these categories: "What I fear most now that my beloved is dead...," 'What I feel stressed about," 'What I dare to hope for..."

Dare to hope? Indeed. Research and experience proves you can not only dare, but expect recovery from and healing of your grief thanks to the simple act of filling these journal pages. In fact, you can count on it.

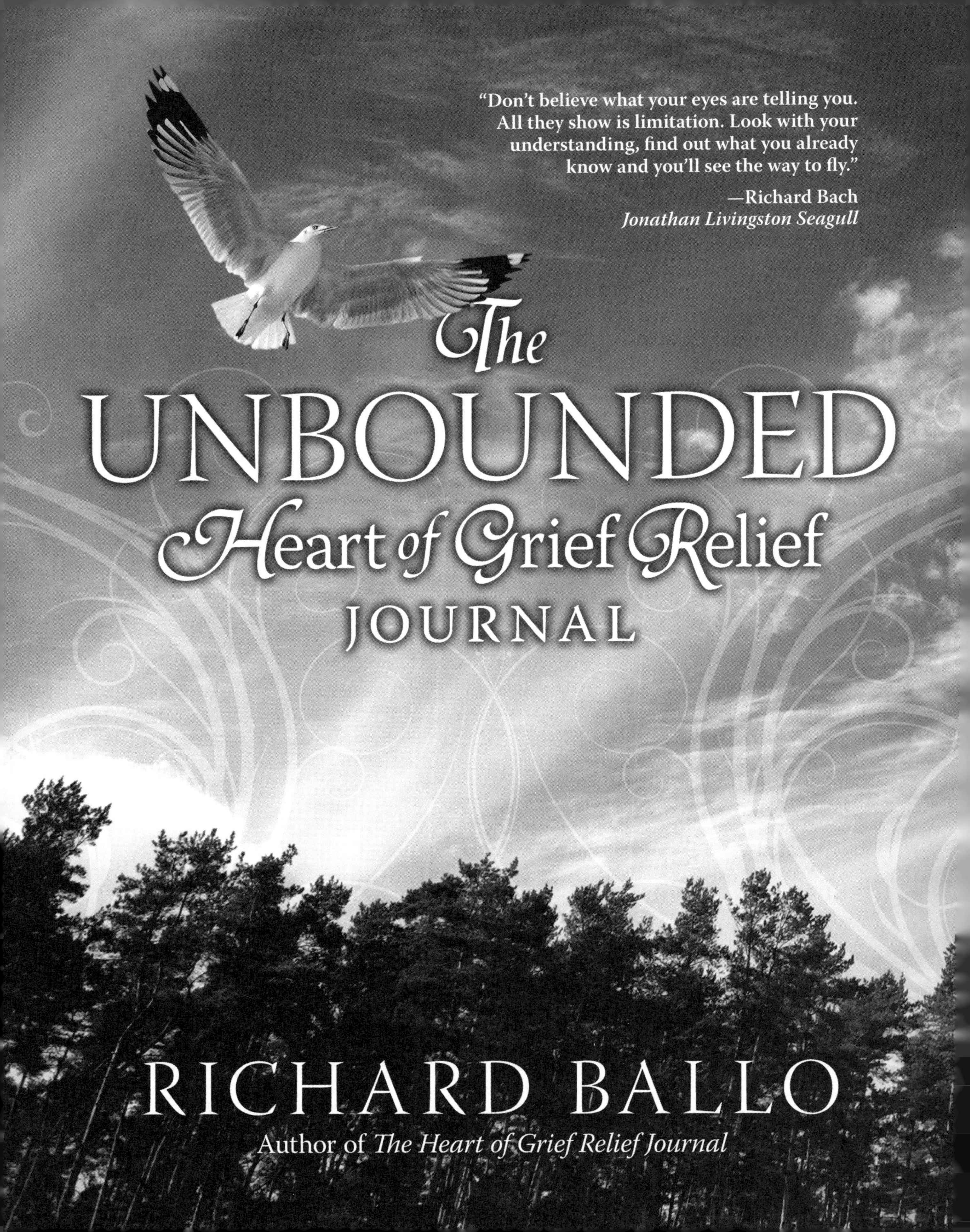
"Don't believe what your eyes are telling you. All they show is limitation. Look with your understanding, find out what you already know and you'll see the way to fly."
—Richard Bach
Jonathan Livingston Seagull
The UNBOUNDED Heart of Grief Relief JOURNAL
RICHARD BALLO
Author of *The Heart of Grief Relief Journal*

“Suffering breaks our world. Like a tree struck by lightning—splintered, shaken, denuded—our world is broken by suffering, and we will never be the same again.”

~Nathan Kollar

"While we are mourning the loss of our friend, others are rejoicing to meet him behind the veil."

~John Taylor

Just One More Day

"...I wish I had just one more day
To see your lovely smile
And hear your laughter fill the air
Just for a little while...
If I could have just one more day
I wouldn't waste a minute
I'd let you know my life's been enriched
By having your love in it..."

~Deborah L. Darling

"How do I know what I think until I see what I say?"

~E. M. Forster

"I found I could say things with color and shapes that I couldn't say any other way—things I had no words for."

~Georgia O'Keefe

"If you think you can, or you think you can't, you're right."
~Henry Ford

“All limitations are self-imposed.”

~Earnest Holmes

"A day at a time, a page at a time, you enter the pages and enter into the flow of life. You are able to ride out the rapids of your life and the quieter waters as well. The pages give you both a place to rest and a vehicle in which to move forward."

~Julia Cameron, *The Artist's Way*

“A friend is like a rainbow.
They brighten your life when you’ve
been through a storm.”

~Anonymous

"I am not a body. I am free.
For I am still as God created me."
~*A Course in Miracles*

"Numbing the pain for a while will
make it worse when you finally feel it."

~Albus Dumbledore in
Harry Potter and the Goblet of Fire by J.K. Rowling

"In the presence of death, my mind had reached its limit and found new freedom. Disillusioned, I discovered hope."

~Sam Keen, philosopher

"If you think you can win, you can win.
Faith is necessary to victory."

~William Hazlitt

"...but no receipt openeth the heart, but a true friend; to whom you may impart griefs, joys, fears, hopes, suspicions, counsels, and whatsoever lieth upon the heart to oppress it..."

~Francis Bacon, *Of Friendship*

"The miracle of life is ageless,
born in time but nourished in eternity."
~A Course in Miracles

"We who lived in concentration camps can remember the men who walked through the huts comforting others, giving away their last piece of bread. They may have been few in number, but they offer sufficient proof that everything can be taken from a man but one thing: the last of the human freedoms—to choose one's attitude in any given set of circumstances, to choose one's own way."

~Viktor Frankl, *Man's Search for Meaning*

"Grief drives men into habits of serious reflection, sharpens the understanding, and softens the heart."

~John Adams

"Not a day passes over the earth but men and women of no note do great deeds, speak great words, and suffer noble sorrows."

~Charles Reade, *The Cloister and the Hearth*

"When pain is to be born, a little courage helps more than much knowledge, a little human sympathy more than much courage, and the least tincture of the love of God more than all."

~C. S. Lewis

"Adversity often activates a strength
we did not know we had."

~Joan Walsh Anglund

"Time does restore to us our quiet joy in the spiritual presence of those we love, so that we learn to remember without pain, and tospeak without choking up with tears…."

~Elisabeth Watson

"...But all our lives we will be subject to sudden small reminders which will bring all the old loss back, overwhelmingly."

~Elisabeth Watson

“It requires more courage to suffer than to die.”
~Napoléon Bonaparte

"That which does not kill me makes me stronger."
~Friedrich Wilhelm Nietzsche, Philosopher

“They that sow in tears, shall reap in joy.”
~The Holy Bible, Psalm 126:5-6

"The Lord God will wipe all
tears from all their faces."

~The Holy Bible, Isaiah 25:8

"Grief knits two hearts in closer bonds than happiness ever can; and common sufferings are far stronger links than common joys."

~Alphonse de Lamartine

"Character cannot be developed in ease and quiet.
Only through experiences of trial and suffering
can the soul be strengthened, vision cleared,
ambition inspired and success achieved."

~Helen Keller

“The difference between stepping stones
and stumbling blocks is how you use them.”

~Anonymous

"Sweet are the uses of adversity which,
like the toad, ugly and venomous,
Wears yet a precious Jewel in his head."

~William Shakespeare, *As You Like It*

"A man does not die of love or his liver
or even of old age; he dies of being a man."

~Miguel de Unamuno

"The caterpillar dies so the butterfly could be born. And, yet, the caterpillar lives in the butterfly and they are but one. So, when I die, it will be that I have been transformed from the caterpillar of earth to the butterfly of the universe."

~John Harricharan

“As I describe the circumstances surrounding her death, tears sting my eyes. In a way, I’m glad I can weep. I’m glad I hurt. These feelings let me know I’m still alive.”

~Richard Ballo, *Life without Lisa*

"Any living thing is in constant change.
This is unavoidable under any circumstance;
it is what life is all about."

~Diana Jacks, *Here to There, Grief to Peace*

"Be kind to yourself. Pamper yourself in any way that isn't self-destructive. Let others help you. Don't expect too much from yourself right now."

~Diana Jacks, Here to There, Grief to Peace

"Short is life, long is love."
~Author unknown

"A human life is a story told by God."
~Hans Christian Andersen

“Don’t forget in the darkness what you learned in the light.”
~Joseph Bayly

"To weep is to make less the depth of grief."
~William Shakespeare, *King Henry the Sixth (VI)*

"It is some relief to weep;
grief is satisfied and carried off by tears."

~Ovid

“Hope is more than a word—it’s a state of being. It’s a firm belief that even if you don’t know how, even if you don’t know when, God will come through and better days are ahead. Life brings rain. Hope dances in the puddles until the sun comes out again.”

~Holley Gerth

"I credit my spiritual journey
for giving me strength to want
to live and love again."
~Sandy Wiltshire, *My Gift of Light*

"...Visual imagery...can sidetrack defenses and 'reality' by tapping directly into the unconscious...(revealing) a visual portrait of... thoughts, feelings and memories."

~Maxine Borowsky Junge,
The Modern History of Art Therapy in the United States

"Make sure to love…Share your love. Show your love. Draw closer, help each other and live your earthly life."

~Sandy Wiltshire, *My Gift of Light*

"A friend is someone who is there
for you when he'd rather be anywhere else."

~Len Wein

"Hiding your feelings or tears and closing yourself off
to other people won't make you stronger or more
responsible; it will only hurt you more in the long run."

~Jenny Wheeler,
Weird Is Normal When Teenagers Grieve

"It is the unknown we fear when we look upon death and darkness, nothing more."

~J.K. Rowling,
Harry Potter and the Half-Blood Prince

"Studies with college students have shown that those who kept journals about their feelings and dreams had more active immune systems and fewer colds than students who didn't keep journals. And the effect persisted up to six months after they stopped keeping their journals."

~Dr. Bernie Siegel, *Bottom Line*

"Don't take it personally if some people—even some of your friends—don't know what to say to you and start to avoid you. Many people feel awkward talking about death."

~Jenny Wheeler,
Weird Is Normal When Teenagers Grieve

"We should talk less and draw more. Personally I would like to renounce speech altogether, and like organic nature, communicate everything I have to say in sketches."

~Johann Wolfgang von Goethe

“We are not human beings having a spiritual experience.
We are spiritual beings having a human experience.”

~Pierre Teilhard de Chardin, theologian

“There is no death!
What seems so is transition;
This life of mortal breath
Is but a suburb of the life elysian,
Whose portal we call Death.”

~Henry W. Longfellow

She is Not Gone

She is not gone
She is the fresh clean scent of spring,
The bluebirds and the song they sing
She is not gone
She is the twinkling stars in the summer sky,
The cool breeze as it passes by
She is not gone
She is the blazing fire on a crisp autumn night
That offers up the warmth and light
She is not gone
She is the snowflakes dancing on a cold winter's day
Beckoning us to come out and play
She is not gone...

~Deborah L. Darling

"Expressing your feelings in the haven of your own journal not only reduces stress and promotes good health, but enables you to understand yourself and make better decisions...Each time you write you have the opportunity to get to know yourself better."

~Dr. Martin G. Groder, *Bottom Line*

"And just at the moment when someone at my side says, 'There, she is gone!' There are other eyes watching her coming, And other voices ready to take up the glad shout, 'Here she comes!' And that is dying."

~Henry Van Dyke, excerpt, *Gone from My Sight*

"Grief is a tidal wave that over takes you, smashes down upon you with unimaginable force, sweeps you up into its darkness, where you tumble and crash against unidentifiable surfaces, only to be thrown out on an unknown beach, bruised, reshaped..."

~Stephanie Ericsson

“There is an alchemy in sorrow. It can be transmuted into wisdom, which, if it does not bring joy, can yet bring happiness.”

~Pearl S. Buck

"Sorrow makes us all children again—destroys all differences of intellect. The wisest know nothing."

~Ralph Waldo Emerson

“How to keep a journal…Don’t just list events. Share feelings, concerns, opinions and reflections on the meaning of your actions.”

~Dr. Martin G. Broder, *Bottom Line*

"It takes time to work through grief, but it is important to go through every thought and feeling because you aren't who you used to be and you must discover who you will be."

~Judith Flinn

"To be able to allow yourself the full immersion into grief will help you in ways that cannot be measured. Those who try avoidance of grief only lengthen the worst of the pain."

~Jill Jacobs, evolvingfaith.blogspot.com

"As we work through our grief and take those first hesitant steps back into life —as we all must eventually do—spirituality can play a significant role in the coping process."

~Sandy Wiltshire, *My Gift of Light*

“The first writing of the human being was drawing, not writing.”
~Marjane Satrapi

"Come, at the shrine of God fervently kneel;
Here bring your wounded hearts;
here tell your anguish;
Earth has no sorrow that heaven cannot heal."

~Thomas Moore, c.1813,
published in Sacred Songs, 1816

"Friends are angels who follow you through life."
~Author Unknown

"Do what you can, with what you have, where you are."

~Teddy Roosevelt

"I was comforted to learn that angels bring healing into our lives, and when needed, a sense of direction. I came to believe they help us, guide us, and want us to understand that heaven is not as far away as we think."

~Sandy Wiltshire, *My Gift of Light*

"My grief attacks were sparked by weird things like the closing of a local amusement park, a microwave oven that stopped working, and trying to decide whether or not to polish my toenails as I got ready to go to a friend's fancy party."

~Jenny Wheeler,
Weird Is Normal When Teenagers Grieve

"If we did all the things we are capable of doing, we would literally astonish ourselves."

~Thomas Edison

"I'm gone now, but I'm still very near.
Death can never separate us.
Each time you feel a gentle breeze,
It's my hand caressing your face.
Each time the wind blows,
It carries my voice whispering your name.
When the wind blows your hair ever so slightly,
Think of it as me pushing a few stray
hairs back in place.
When you feel a few raindrops fall on your face,
It's me placing soft kisses.
At night look up in the sky and see the stars
shining so brightly.
I'm one of those stars and I'm winking at you and smiling with delight.
For never forget you're the apple of my eye."

~Mary M. Green

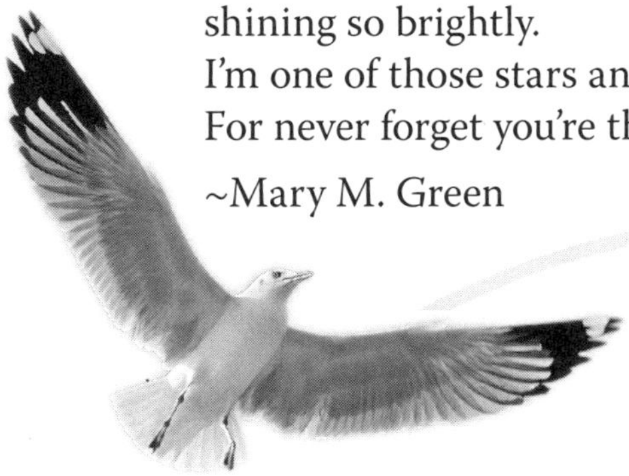

"Accept your mortality. When you accept that you're going to die someday, your time, activities and feelings will become more significant. You'll see the value of living in the present and will be more likely to resolve problems."

~Dr. Bernie Siegel, *Bottom Line*

"You will lose someone you can't live without, and your heart will be badly broken, and the bad news is that you never completely get over the loss of your beloved. But this is also the good news. They live forever in your broken heart that doesn't seal back up. And you come through. It's like having a broken leg that never heals perfectly—that still hurts when the weather gets cold, but you learn to dance with the limp."

~Anne Lamott

"There is but one freedom, to put oneself right with death. After that everything is possible. I cannot force you to believe in God. Believing in God amounts to coming to terms with death. When you have Accepted death, the problem of God will be solved—and not the reverse."

~Albert Camus

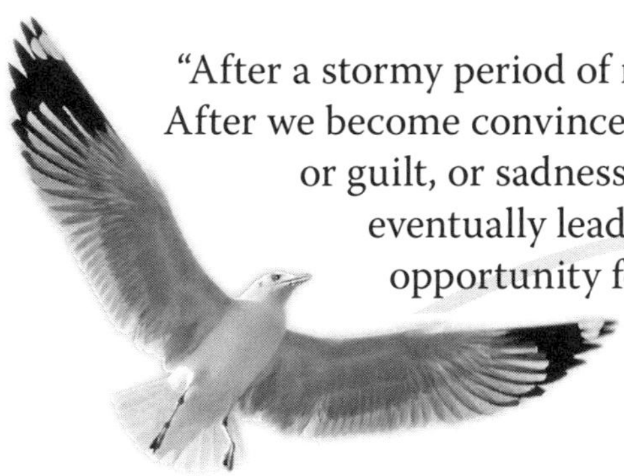

"After a stormy period of mixed feelings of prolonged sadness there comes a calm. After we become convinced that we are at the very brink of eternal despair, or fear, or guilt, or sadness, we are given a reprieve. We have a breathing space that eventually leads to whole days that have personal value and offer us the opportunity for affection. Then we recognize that no period of misery is endless and unrelenting; it is instead, changeable."

~Carol Staudacher

“Grief does not change you....It reveals you.”
~John Green, *The Fault in Our Stars*

"Only people who are capable of
loving strongly can also suffer great sorrow,
but this same necessity of loving serves to
counteract their grief and heals them."

~Leo Tolstoy

“Man, when he does not grieve, hardly exists.”

~Antonio Porchia, Voces, 1943,
translated from Spanish by W.S. Merwin

"I still miss those I loved who are no longer with me but I find I am grateful for having loved them. The gratitude has finally conquered the loss."

~Rita Mae Brown

"Volunteer. People who give an hour or more a week to a good cause have fewer illnesses and live longer than people who do not. Being involved in an altruistic way with other people, your community, the world—learning to give rather than take—becomes part of a pattern that makes you healthier."

~Dr. Bernie Siegel, *Bottom Line*

"No one wants to die. Even people who want to go to heaven don't want to die to get there. And yet death is a destination we all share. No one has ever escaped it."

~Steve Jobs

"Your time is limited, so don't waste it.... Don't be trapped by dogma.... Don't let the noise of other's opinions drown out your own inner voice. And most important, have the courage to follow your heart and intuition...."

~Steve Jobs

"Every person, all the events of your life are
there because you have drawn them there.
What you choose to do with them is up to you."

~Richard Bach, *Illusions*

"Getting blind-sided (by grief) happens
to everyone. It will keep on happening.
But the down time will get shorter,
the pain less intense and you'll be able
to bounce back sooner."

~Diana Jacks, *Here to There, Grief to Peace*

"...you don't have to get over your loss according to any certain time table...
you always have the right to grieve and to need comfort from others."

~Jenny Wheeler,
Weird Is Normal When Teenagers Grieve

"White snows of winter
Falling in silence
Weave a soft coverlet spotless and deep
Fold it over her...gently...ah gently
She who was lovely has fallen asleep..."

~author unknown

"The soul would have no rainbow, had the eyes no tears."
~John Vance Cheney

“Don’t believe what your eyes are telling you. All they show is limitation. Look with your understanding, find out what you already know and you’ll see the way to fly.”

~Richard Bach, *Jonathan Livingston Seagull*

The Heart of Grief Relief Kit

Think of this as a first aid kit for your grieving heart. This unique bereavement kit contains a variety of things to aid you on your healing path until you finally do achieve relief from grief.

This kit was conceived by Richard Ballo who at age 39, lost his wife Lisa to cancer. Their two sons were only 5 and six at the time of mom's death.

Since nothing like *The Heart of Grief Relief Kit* existed, he obviously could not take advantage of it. But various components of the kit were available to him, and he used them to great advantage. He offers this assemblage to you to speed and ensure your own recovery.

Designed to help you:

- *Work through your grief.*
- *Find peace at the end of your healing from grief journey.*
- *Move beyond your loss.*
- *Embrace the pain in order to open your heart.*
- *Work through and banish feelings of helplessness, disorientation, utter despair and numbness.*
- *Get on with your life.*
- *Embrace the new, albeit different, life that lies before you.*

The Kit Components:

The Heart of Grief Relief Journal–a journal, a book, an inspiration, a resource guide all rolled into one. Journaling is an invaluable healing tool, and it was pivotal to Rich's recovery. Here is more than a journal–a balm for your soul.

Life without Lisa–This award-winning book candidly chronicles Rich Ballo's healing journey that spans the five years following his wife Lisa's death. Its pages reveal the depths of Rich's despair and his ultimate healing. It will reassure you that whatever you are feeling is normal and that the road to grief relief will take many twists and turns–but that you absolutely can get there from here.

Grief Relief Stress Heart–Keep this squeezable heart handy at your desk or wherever you most frequently are. The heart shape reminds you that the path to grief relief is through your heart. Squeezing this heart provides an escape valve for tensions you may feel.

Grief Relief Door Hanger–This handy alert can be kept on the doorknob to your office or bedroom–or whatever room you prefer. It acknowledges that some days will be better than others, and this can silently and effectively alert others whether or not it is a good day to enter or to let you suffer a grief attack in private. One side of the door hanger invites the visitor in. The other side may be displayed when you truly want to be alone. It warns that a grief attack is in process, please do not disturb.

Grief Relief Heart Key Ring–This key ring serves a dual purpose: to remind you that the path to grief relief truly does run through your heart and that you may be delighted at the benefits you receive when you jump in the car and drive to Hospice for group and/or private bereavement counseling.

Ball Point Journal Pen–This ball point *Heart of Grief Relief* pen may be used to write in your journal to express your deepest concerns and feelings.

When You Are Grieving Booklet–*When You Are Grieving* is an easy-to-read, gentle guide to healing for people who have suffered the death of a loved one. It not only reassures, soothes and guides adults struggling with grief, but also includes special tips for children and teens. It clearly explains the grieving process in an extremely helpful way. This booklet helps those left behind to better understand their grief, find comfort, and move forward with hope.

The Heart of Grief Relief Kit--$34.94

Each kit includes:

- *The Heart of Grief Relief Journal*
- *Life without Lisa*
- Grief Relief Squeezable Stress Heart
- Grief Relief Door Hanger
- Grief Relief Heart Key Ring
- Grief Relief Journal Pen
- *When You Are Grieving* booklet

(All kit components come packages in a sturdy plastic bad with the Heart of Grief Relief logo on the front. You can add your own custom labels to the front of the bag when you order ten or more kits.)

To order the Kit call 239-404-6739 or email info@tolmainmainpress.com.

Questions regarding quantity discounts may be directed to info@tolmanmainpress.com, or tmp758@comcast.net.